ROAM-ANTS

Benjamin Lachapelle

BEN ANIMALIA BOOKS
16445 rue de l'Esplanade, Mirabel, Quebec, Canada J7N 3E4
All rights reserved

Roam-Ants
Copyright © 2024 by Benjamin Lachapelle
Thank you for purchasing this book, supporting
an autistic author and illustrator and
for complying with copyright laws by not reproducing,
scanning, or distributing any part of it in any form without permission.
Copyright encourages diverse voices.

Library and Archives Canada
ISBN: 978-1-7386878-4-8

For information, please contact Ben.Animalia@outlook.com
or visit www.BenAnimalia.com

Dedicated to my friends
Carly Hay and Lena Baldoni

This book challenges the values we place on relationship status and notions of happiness and well-being.

Roam-Ants invites you to consider a more INCLUSIVE perspective and embrace all the meaningful ways a happy and independent life can be lived.

Romance

Noun   ro·mance | rō-ˌman(t)s

An expression of love

Action or feeling of caring or affection

A love story

Roam-Ants

Ants who march to the beat
of their own hearts.

Roam, discover and love yourself,
because happiness comes from within.

FOREWORD

By Dr. Yuthika Girme
Associate Professor at Simon Fraser University

Once upon time, I fell in love with relationship psychology. How do people live happily ever after in their relationships? I spent years trying to understand Romance. Over the years, I came to the realization that I may have been asking the wrong question all along. To truly understand the key to happiness we first need to understand how people build a relationship with themselves; it all starts with Roam-Ants.

When I first read Benjamin Lachapelle's book about Roam-Ants, all I could do was smile ear to ear because Benjamin was preaching (or rather, drawing and writing) to the choir! As a singlehood and relationship psychologist, my research aims to understand what makes single and coupled people feel secure and satisfied in their lives. Some of my research has shown how much pressure society can put on people to find "the one" and how isolating this messaging can be for single people (truly, Interfear-Ants!).

Roam-Ants tells a real and honest story about peoples' journey to build a happy and meaningful life. Benjamin gently guides readers to question the assumption that people have to be in a romantic relationship to be truly happy. Through his creative illustrations and knowledge of the animal world Benjamin highlights how singlehood is a common, valid, and meaningful experience.

Benjamin illustrates the diverse ways in which people experience love as a single person. He tells a story of how people can love themselves by pursuing things that bring them joy – in ways that are simple and routine, as well as in ways that are intricate and grand. Benjamin also makes it clear that being single doesn't mean being alone. Family, friends, and community offer single people important sources of love and support.

Many of the messages in Roam-Ants about self love, happiness, and friendship dovetail beautifully with what singlehood and relationship psychologists are more recently learning about single life. But, here is this amazing young person figuring it out for themselves and sharing a positive and inclusive message about singlehood with the world!

As you read Roam-Ants, I hope you feel as inspired as I felt reading this funny, witty, and joyful book. I hope you feel inspired to do what you love, inspired to love yourself, and inspired to pursue your happily, ever after… full of Roam-Ants.

Everyone wants to have
a happy and meaningful life.

Some think the only way to be happy is to have a romantic partner.

To find someone special

A soulmate

And be "in love"

But,
is romantic love the only way
to true happiness?

NO

In life, there are many roads
to a happy, fulfilling and rich life.

In the animal world,
there is great diversity.

There are different ways of being.

Some animals

mate for life.

In fact, ~90% of birds

pair up for life.

But single life is also very common for many species.

In fact, ~97% of mammals live very content and peaceful solo lives.

So, a happy life is possible with or without a partner.

How can you find happiness which is meaningful for you?

How do you connect all the pieces?

And solve the puzzle of your life.

The answer is to have
ROAM-ANTS.

Lots and lots of roam-ants!

Roam-ants help you learn to love and value yourself.

Roam-ants show you that
true happiness is
not found in another.

It is found in you!

Those with roam-ants fill up with self-love!

And live a joyful life!

Roam-ants encourage you to pursue passions, hobbies and special interests.

Fall in love with what you love!

Fall in love with nature.

And marvel with roam-ants
at the quiet wonders around you.

Fall in love with your favorite books.

Your favorite movies

Favorite songs or bands

Favorite places

Favorite foods, games or things

Having roam-ants will help you
figure out what brings
joy and meaning to you
and what makes your life richer.

Explore and discover yourself!

Roam the world with roam-ants!

Take your roam-ants and go on adventures!

Swim in the ocean

Run through the trees

Fall asleep under the stars

And catch the sunrise
from magical places…

or from ordinary places.

Let the wonders of nature fill your soul!

Let roam-ants help you achieve inner peace.

Everyone needs peace and contentment to be truly happy.

You don't need to hope
and pray to find a soulmate.

Roam-ants will show you that soulmates can be amazing family or friends.

The kind you can call anytime about anything.

Family or friends who can share all your big ideas and values with.

And give you support
and true friendship.

A soulmate can also be your pet.

Many people have deep connections with their pets.

And with animals in the wild.

Let roam-ants show you that

you are never alone.

Life can have ups and downs.

Roam-ants will ride with you and make sure you're having fun along the way.

Roam-ants will help you get over the cracks and crevices of your life.

Try new things and
soar as high as you want
with roam-ants!

Roam-ants will help you focus and reflect on what matters to you.

And who matters to you.

Become the happiest version of you!

For you!

The opposite of roam-ants are
INTERFEAR-ANTS!

They will stick their
noses in your life.

Beware of interfear-ants!

Interfear-ants will try to scare you into believing that you will never be happy without a romantic partner!

That being single is
a terrible thing!

Having roam-ants will block out those interfear-ants!

And help build the
right connections for you.

So you can live a joyful and harmonious independent life.

Let roam-ants help you become the writer of your own story.

Conductor of
your own orchestra.

Ringmaster in the circus of your life.

And sing the songs that speak to your heart.

No matter what happens, love the world.

And be gentle on yourself.

All you need is love...

and roam-ants.

Many autistic individuals take things literally because they are
LITERAL THINKERS.

This book is about cultivating self-love & romance/roam-ants from the perspective of Benjamin Lachapelle, an autistic artist & author-illustrator.

As always, this project is a loving collaboration between Benjamin and his mother.

ACKNOWLEDGMENTS

This book was inspired by many of Ben's good friends in the disability community. They are shining examples of how to live authentic, happy and creative lives with big open-hearts. As neurodivergent individuals, their perspectives are truly unique and they don't always live by traditional norms. Because let's face it, "normal" isn't for everyone.

Dear Friends, thank you for investing in your independence and personal growth. By building meaningful friendships and thriving in your best single lives, you are proving that happiness and well-being is possible for everyone and changing the deficit narrative of single life. Wishing you much love and roam-ants!

Thank you to our family, friends and supporters who have greatly encouraged Ben throughout his life. It truly takes a village, and we've been blessed by knowing the best villagers!

Enormous thanks to *Inspirations Newspaper* and *Inspirations Entrepreneurial Award* sponsor Henry Zavriyev for financial assistance in making this first publication of *Roam-Ants* possible.

If you enjoyed **ROAM-ANTS**, check out **PACE-ANTS** (a book about *PATIENCE*)!

Follow @BenAnimalia for more information on upcoming books in **The ANTS Series!**

ALSO BY BENJAMIN LACHAPELLE

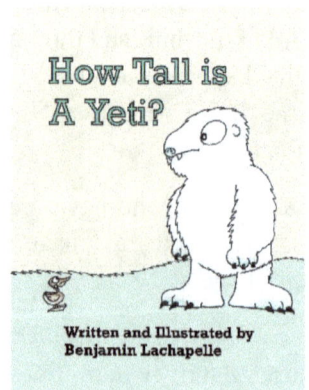

<u>The Yeti Series</u>
How Tall is a Yeti?
How Loud is a Yeti?
Who Has Spaghetti for the Yeti?
The Yeti's Favorite Colors
The Yeti's Footprints
Halloween Yeti
Merry Christmas Yeti
How Fast is a Yeti?
The Yeti and His Teddy

The Olympic Zoo
Zoo Dance

Benjamin Lachapelle is a Canadian autistic artist born & raised in the Laurentians, Quebec. He is a painter, sculptor & author-illustrator of children's books. His passion for animals is the singular focus of his work, which has been presented in numerous exhibitions & festivals. Ben loves his community & donates much of his time to local causes.

 @benanimalia

Benjamin Lachapelle is the inspiration for **Ben Animalia**, a social enterprise which promotes wildlife protection, conservation, neurodiversity, autism and disability awareness, acceptance and inclusion.

Please visit **www.BenAnimalia.com** or follow @benanimalia for more information.

Ben Animalia Books

Thank you for your support!

www.ingramcontent.com/pod-product-compliance
Lightning Source LLC
LaVergne TN
LVHW021602070426
835507LV00015B/1902